NUMEROLOGY

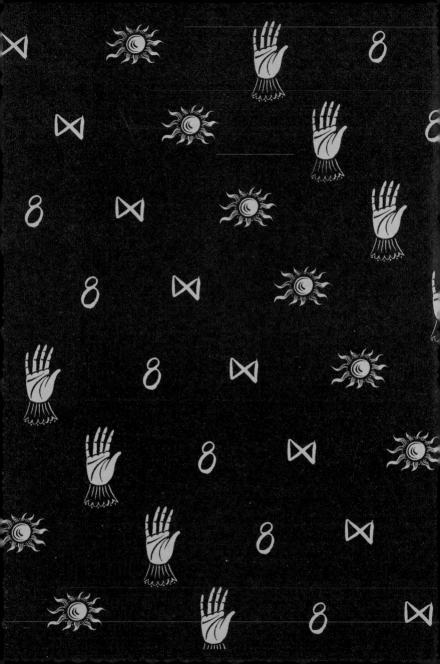

NUMEROLOGY

PATRICIA FARRELL

ELEMENT

Shaftesbury, Dorset • Rockport, Massachusetts • Melbourne, Victoria

© Element Books Limited 1997

First published in Great Britain by
ELEMENT BOOKS LIMITED
Shaftesbury, Dorset SP7 8BP

Published in the USA in 1997 by
ELEMENT BOOKS INC.
PO Box 830, Rockport, MA 01966

Published in Australia in 1997 by
ELEMENT BOOKS LIMITED
and distributed by Penguin Australia Ltd
487 Maroondah Highway, Ringwood, Victoria 3134

Designed and created with
THE BRIDGEWATER BOOK COMPANY

Printed and bound in Singapore

British Library Cataloguing in Publication data available

Library of Congress Cataloging in Publication data available

ISBN: 1 86204 132 6

ELEMENT BOOKS LIMITED
Editorial Director *Julia McCutchen*
Managing Editor *Caro Ness*
Project Editor *Allie West*
Production Director *Roger Lane*
Production *Sarah Golden*

THE BRIDGEWATER BOOK COMPANY
Art Director *Peter Bridgewater*
Designer *Stephen Minns*
Managing Editor *Anne Townley*
Project Editor *Caroline Earle*
Picture Research *Julia Hanson*

Computer Illustrations *Ivan Hissey*
Endpapers *Sarah Young*

Picture credits:
The Bodleian Library, Oxford: front cover, 8, 13. The Bridgeman Art Library,
London: Prado, Madrid – Claudio Coello, *The Triumph of St Augustine* 9, The
Courtauld Institute, Lucas Cranach, *Adam and Eve* 11. e.t. archive: 7, 51, 54.
Images, the Charles Walker Collection: 21, 25, 55. Rex Features: 31, 33, 38, 41,
43, 45, 52. Werner Forman Archive: National Museum of Anthropology, Mexico,
front cover and 6(L). Zefa: 35, 37, 49, 50(B).

*There are many different views and interpretations of numerology, some of
which may conflict with each other. This book represents the author's interpretation
of the philosophy, based on her own information, knowledge, and experience. The
book is also a condensed and simplified form of what can be a complex system.*

CONTENTS

WHAT IS NUMEROLOGY?

Numerology is the study of numbers and their symbolic significance. It is a philosophy that does not contradict or reinforce the beliefs of any religion, nor does it claim to predict the future. The practice is simply concerned with gaining a deeper knowledge of the patterns of life.

HOW TO USE NUMEROLOGY

Every number has its own significance. Understanding their individual meaning, and how their power and potential relate to us personally, can help improve our comprehension of our own selves considerably.

Numbers affect every area of our lives. We use them to define ourselves and our place in the world. Currency, time, and bank details are factors that govern daily life, and all rely on the application of numbers. In numerology, however, the most significant numbers are your date of birth and the numbers that relate to the particular letters of your name.

WHY USE NUMBERS?

Numerologists believe numbers are the only constants in a world that is continually changing and open to interpretation. For example, one person's view of a mountain may differ from another's, and although the mountain may exist for centuries, it is forever changing. But numbers remain the same for every person in the world. A number cannot be anything other than it is.

PERSONAL NUMBERS, LIKE BIRTHDATES, CAN OFFER PERSONAL INSIGHT.

NUMEROLOGY IS CENTURIES OLD.
GODS AND ANIMALS SYMBOLIZE A
DATE IN THIS MAYAN CARVING.

THE ORIGINS
OF NUMEROLOGY

3 Numerology is reputed to be one of the oldest analytical techniques in the world. Some writers claim it derived mainly from ancient Hindu and Arabic teachings, but it was also part of the Greek,

Babylonian, Hebrew, and Chinese tradition. Two and a half thousand years ago, Egyptian and Babylonian priests used numerology as a way of understanding their fellow man. The Chaldeans, Mayans, Tibetans, Phoenicians, and Celts are also believed to have developed their own systems of numerology in order to understand nature.

A SACRED SCIENCE

5 For centuries, numbers were perceived as the building blocks from which the universe is constructed. Numbers were used to explain the rhythms of nature and the story of creation. The sacred rituals of the Celts were often based on numbers. Greek philosophers equated studying numbers with studying the power of God, and Jewish students of the Qabalah devised their own doctrine of numbers. Even the Bible has its Book of Numbers.

TO ANCIENT EGYPTIAN PRIESTS,
NUMBERS WERE SIGNIFICANT TO
PSYCHOLOGICAL UNDERSTANDING.

NUMEROLOGY TODAY

9 Much of the numerology prac-
ticed in the West today is based
on the philosophy of Pythagoras. But there are many interpretations of numerology.
Even among Pytha-
gorean numerologists,
there are differences
of interpretation,
that have arisen as
individual students
gradually developed
their own systems.

*Egyptian
priest*

*Image of god
Amon*

Hieroglyphics

ANCIENT PHILOSOPHERS DEVELOPED
THEORIES OF NUMEROLOGY.

KEY FIGURES

2 The ancient Greek philosophers, Socrates and Aristotle, used numerology. In the Christian church, St. Augustine was fascinated by numbers and spent much of his time studying their religious significance. Eminent twentieth-century psychologist, Carl Jung, believed that a number is "quantity as well as meaning." The Greek mathematician and philosopher, Pythagoras, *(582–507 B.C.E.)* was the father of numbers, and the most important figure in numerology. According to Pythagoras, "everything is number and to know numbers is to know thyself." He also claimed that "number is the law of the universe." Although there are other numerological systems, the Pythagorean formula for calculating personal name numbers is the most popular and widely used today *(see pages 20–1)*. However, Pythagoras left only fragmented details of his workings of numerology, which may account for the many differences in numerological interpretation today.

Plato *(c. 427–347 B.C.E.)* was fascinated by numbers because he claimed they are eternal and universal. Plato believed numbers were the only things we could really know, because we use our reason to understand them. Everything else we perceive with our senses. According to Plato, we cannot truly know what we perceive because everyone can have a different perception. Only what we know through reason is eternal and universal.

ST. AUGUSTINE APPLIED THE
PRACTICE OF NUMEROLOGY TO
HIS CHRISTIAN BELIEFS.

THE POWER OF NUMBERS

4 There are two basic beliefs in numerology. One, that life is cyclical rather than linear; two, that the world is dynamic. It is alive with vibrating energy, and everything within the world also vibrates with that energy. Numbers are seen as symbols of this constant cycle of energy. They reveal the patterns of life itself.

Each number has its own vibration and represents character, power, potential, and opportunities. According to numerologists, the power and potential of everything within nature, including ourselves, can be better understood through the detailed study of numbers.

ODD AND EVEN NUMBERS HAVE OPPOSITE, BALANCING QUALITIES.

THE SEARCH FOR BALANCE

6 Numbers are divided into the two complementary opposite groups of masculine and feminine. Odd numbers such as one, three, five, seven, and nine, are believed to possess a masculine energy. The even numbers of two, four, six, eight, and ten are in the feminine group.

In traditional Chinese numerology, odd numbers are "yang," and masculine; these numbers relate to the heavens, and are believed to bring good fortune. Even numbers are "yin," and feminine; these numbers relate to the earth, and represent receptivity.

These opposites work together. No number is an isolated unit, since every one has its complementary shadow number *(see page 16)*. It is the interplay between masculine and feminine, and complementary opposites, that provides the basis of all creativity, including life itself.

NUMEROLOGISTS BELIEVE NUMBERS HOLD
THE KEY TO ALL HUMAN LIFE, SHAPING
EXISTENCE FROM ITS VERY BEGINNINGS.

NUMEROLOGY AND YOU

7 The numbers in your life are not arbitrary. They are part of your life plan, and they are therefore of great significance to you. Everyone has a unique arrangement of numbers, that act as a guide, but do not control your life.

A professional numerology reading may reveal several numbers of significance in your life, but the two numbers most important for personal development are your personal birthdate number and your personal name number *(see pages 14–25)*.

WHICH NUMBERS?

9 The numbers used in numerology are mainly the "primary integers," that is, numbers one to nine. In order to compile your own numerological chart, every number is reduced to a single digit by using a simple formula that involves adding the numbers together *(see pages 14–29)*.

Each of the numbers between one and nine has a meaning *(see pages 30–47)*. Each letter of the alphabet also has a numerical value between one and nine. Pythagoras used the numbers one to nine to measure the cycles of life; in modern numerology, they are used to guide us toward personal fulfillment.

MASTER NUMBERS

8 Some numbers are not usually reduced to a single digit. These are the numbers 11, 22, and 33. They are known as master numbers. Master numbers are believed to have a special significance, because the person to whom they apply has a special lesson to learn or role to play in this life.

But the demands of the master number can also be difficult to live up to. If you have a master number and you find it too demanding to cope with, you can reduce your burden by adding the digits of your master number together to form a single number.

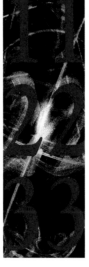

MASTER NUMBERS
CONTAIN UNIQUE
POWERS.

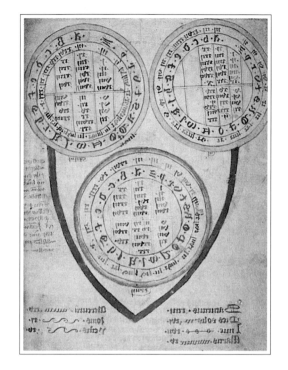

NUMEROLOGY IS A SIGNIFICANT
FEATURE IN THIS 14TH-CENTURY
FORTUNE-TELLING TRACT.

NUMBER PROFILES

4 The number profiles, that start on *page 30*, give a brief introduction to the energies and potentials of the numbers one to nine, and the master numbers. Use these profiles as a reference for the potential of your personal birthdate number and your name number. They will reveal your positive and negative qualities. The objective is to become aware of your negative qualities and to make them more positive, and to know your positive qualities and build on them.

YOUR PERSONAL BIRTHDATE AND NAME NUMBER

Your personal birthdate number is sometimes called your life path number. It is derived from the numbers that make up your birthdate, and is the most important number in your life.

ITS MEANING AND PURPOSE

Your personal birthdate number represents your potential. How you relate to your personal number both determines, and is reflected in, how well you fulfill your potential in life.

You must not think that you are restricted or governed by this number. Like all numbers, it is simply a tool that you can use to dig deeper into self-knowledge in order to grow, express yourself, and open up to the many possibilities that life has to offer you.

At critical times in life, your birthdate number can also provide useful guidance. If you feel lost, indecisive, or directionless, you can call on your birthdate number.

HOW TO WORK OUT YOUR NUMBER

To work out your number, add together the number of the day, month, and year of your birth, until you arrive at a single digit.

For example, if your date of birth is March 21, 1959 (21/3/1959) add together:

2+1=3

+3=6

+1+9+5+9=30

3+0=3

YOUR PERSONAL BIRTHDATE NUMBER IS 3

BIRTHDATES HOLD THE
KEY TO UNDERSTANDING
OUR CAPABILITIES.

THE VALUE OF SHADOW NUMBERS

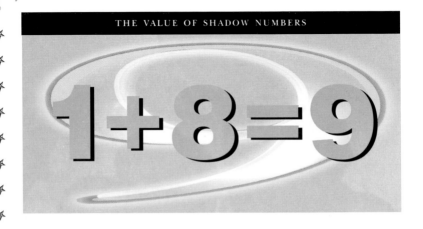

YOUR SHADOW NUMBER

In the same way that physical objects cast a shadow, numerologists believe that numbers also have a shadow. A shadow number is not evil or sinister though, it simply refers to the hidden qualities and potential of a number. In fact, a shadow number is a number's complementary opposite.

HOW IT WORKS WITH YOUR BIRTHDATE NUMBER

Your birthdate number represents your future potential and the possibilities that life holds for you. Your shadow number represents the qualities that are deep within you and the characteristics that you have inherited that define your personality.

THE VALUE OF SHADOW NUMBERS

Your birthdate number and its shadow number always add up to 9. To find your shadow number, subtract your birthdate number from 9. The shadow number of 9 is 9, because the sum 18 also gives 9 (1+8=9). Numerologists believe that the shadow number balances your birthdate number. It is believed to be most active in the second and third stages of life, when we naturally tend to become more introspective and curious about our inner selves.

SHADOW NUMBER

	EMOTIONAL LOVE	
	2	
INDIVIDUAL GOOD	COLLECTIVE GOOD	WISDOM
4	5	6
	SPIRITUAL ACHIEVEMENT	SERVICE
	8	9

A NUMBER FOR EACH STAGE OF YOUR LIFE

5 Many cultures believe that we live out our lives in stages or cycles. Numerologists believe there are three major stages in life, each containing nine nine-year life cycles. Each stage relates to a particular number that forms part of your birthdate number. The three key numbers are your birth day number, your birth month number, and your birth year number.

TO WORK OUT THE STAGES

8 Going back to our original personal birthdate example (21/3/1959) you can see how this is worked out:

Birth day (21st)	= 2+1	=	**3**
Birth month (March)		=	**3**
Birth year (1959)	= 1+9+5+9		
	= (24) 2+4		
		=	**6**

These numbers represent the three stages of life *(see opposite)*.

THE THREE STAGES OF LIFE

☾ 1. *The birth day number represents the first stage of life, that is the first 27 years. The number three in the example (far left), and its shadow number of six, would be most active during this time.*

☾ 2. *The birth month number represents the second stage of life, that is the next 27 years. This is usually a transitionary period between the physical and emotional concerns of early life, and the more contemplative nature of mid- to later life.*

☾ 3. *The birth year number represents the third stage, that lasts from around the age of 54 until death. It is a period of love, spirituality, and wisdom. The number six in the example, and its shadow three, would be most active during this time.*

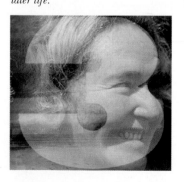

YOUR PERSONAL NAME NUMBER

5 In numerology, every name has a number. Most people consider their name to be nothing more than a label, but according to the ancient mystical idea of naming, your secret or true name is a personal talisman that protects your identity.

ITS IMPORTANCE AND MEANING

1 To a numerologist, the name is significant because it was given to us by the generation before, and so holds a vibration of what we have inherited. In a sense our name reveals three numbers – the vowels add up to a number that reveals the potential of the soul or psyche, the consonants reveal the personality, and the two together reveal our overall self-expression.

- *The soul or psyche is the real you – your conscience and wisdom. In numerology, the soul is believed to "inherit" qualities from previous incarnations.*
- *The personality is the way other people see you, the image you present to the world.*
- *The overall number reveals how the qualities of the soul, and the potential of the personality, combine in the way we express ourselves.*

HOW TO WORK OUT YOUR NAME NUMBER

4 The Pythagorean system is the easiest and most popular way of working out the numerical value of each letter:
- Write out your full name and give the appropriate number to each letter using the chart opposite. Add the numbers together until you arrive at a single digit or a master number. For example, William Shakespeare would work out his name number as shown on *page 23*.

THE PYTHAGOREAN SYSTEM

1 2 3 4 5 6 7 8 9

A B C D E F G H I

J K L M N O P Q R

S T U V W X Y Z

WILLIAM SHAKESPEARE
5 9 3 3 9 1 4   1 8 1 2 5 1 7 5 1 9 5

$5+9+3+3+9+1+4 = 34$	$1+8+1+2+5+1+7+5+1+9+5 = 45$
$3+4 = 7$	$4+5 = 9$
$7+9 = 16$	
$1+6 = 7$	

His personal name number is 7, the number of the thinker, wise teacher, and communicator.

To work out your soul number simply add the values of all the vowels in your name. For William Shakespeare that would be:

$9+9+1=19=1+9=10=1+0$	$= 1$
$1+5+5+1+5 = 17= 1+7$	$= 8$
$1+8$	$= 9$
Soul number	$= 9$

For your personality number, add the consonants together. For William Shakespeare this would be:

$5+3+3+4= 15=1+5$	$= 6$
$1+8+2+1+7+9=28=2+8=10=1+0$	$= 1$
$6+1$	$= 7$
Personality number	$= 7$

YOUR MANY NAMES

Your name number helps you understand more about yourself, but it is not as significant as your birthdate number. One reason for this is that your name can change. You can alter it by law or by marriage, or people can address you by a nickname, pet name, or a distorted version of your full name. A birthdate, however, is tamperproof. If you were born on May 7, 1955, nothing can change that fact.

WHICH NAME IS REALLY YOU?

If you have several names it is difficult to know your true personal name number. The name that is of initial numerological interest is the name on your birth certificate. But the name you use and respond to most often is the name most representative of you at the moment. Use it to discover the present numerological potential of your name. If you are more often known as Mrs. Jones rather than Sarah Jones, use the numerical values of the letters M, R, and S.

WHICH NUMBER SHOULD YOU BE GUIDED BY?

Be guided first and foremost by your personal birthdate number. But do pay attention to your personal name number, especially if it is the same as your birthdate number, the same as your shadow number, or if it offers potentials in life that are not part of your personal birthdate number.

THE NINE NUMBERS SIGNIFICANT TO HUMANS ARE LINKED TO THE NINE ASTROLOGICAL SPHERES.

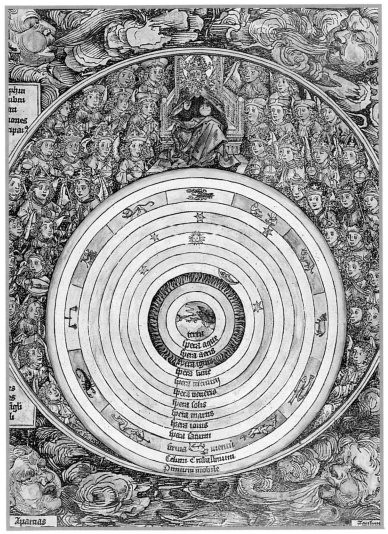

NUMBERS FOR
THE YEAR AHEAD

Numerologists maintain that there is a correct time for everything we plan and do – a project succeeds only if it is put into practice when the time is right. The positive side of that belief is that you can achieve anything you want in life if, by understanding the significance of your personal numbers, you are attuned to time, and are able to recognize the opportunities it presents and act upon them accordingly.

Some people know instinctively when the time is right to act. In fact, most of us at some time are prompted by intuition, but it may happen very rarely.

Numerologists believe that understanding the potential of numbers can help us to capitalize on our intuition, so that we can recognize the right time and so enjoy more successful endeavors.

THE UNIVERSAL NUMBER

Every year has a universal number, that represents the potential that exists in the world for that year. Based on the belief that space is not a vacuum but a place of swirling, vibrant energy, the universal number of the year represents the enormous potential that is available to each and every one of us in the coming year.

TO CALCULATE THE UNIVERSAL NUMBER

To calculate the number of the year ahead, simply add together all the digits of that year. Each year has its own number, but there is also a dominant number for each decade and each century.

HOW TO CALCULATE THE UNIVERSAL YEAR NUMBER

$$1997 = 1+9+9+7 = 26 = 2+6 = 8$$

$$1998 = 1+9+9+8 = 27 = 2+7 = 9$$

$$1999 = 1+9+9+9 = 28 = 2+8 = 10 \ (1+0) = 1$$

$$2000 = 2+0+0+0 = 2$$

$$2001 = 2+0+0+1 = 3$$

A quick look at the five-year chart above reveals important key points. The 1990s were years when the numbers one and nine were dominant. The number one is the number of materialism; it has a dynamic masculine energy. The number nine is associated with law, discrimination, and judgment, although it is also the number that has the potential for humanitarianism and spiritual growth. Both numbers one and nine have paved the way for the number two, that will be the dominant number in the twenty-first century. The number two has a feminine energy. This energy is now manifesting itself as women are becoming more active in world affairs and men are getting more in touch with their feminine side. Number two is also the number of cooperation, communication, sensitivity, and peace-making.

YOUR PERSONAL YEAR

The number of the universal year symbolizes the potential that exists around you, potential on which you can rely if the time is right. But there is also a personal year number, that relates to the potential within you. Your personal year number can point you in the right direction for personal growth and self-discovery throughout the coming year.

HOW TO CALCULATE YOUR PERSONAL YEAR NUMBER

It is easy to work out your personal number for the year ahead. For example, returning to the birthdate we used earlier – March 21, 1959 – we can calculate the potential of 1997 for the owner of this birthdate simply by adding the birth day number and the birth month number to 1997.

For example:

(21st) = 2+1 = 3

+ (March) 3

+ 1+9+9+7

= 3+3+1+9+9+7

= 32 = 3+2

= 5

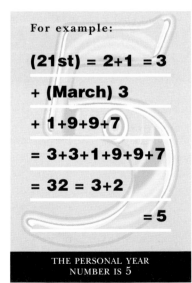

THE PERSONAL YEAR NUMBER IS 5

WHICH NUMBER?

5 Your personal year number is likely to differ from the universal year number. In this case, compare the potential and influences of both numbers. You may be able to draw on the power of both; perhaps the influences of one can support those of the other. If the numbers appear to be in conflict, you must decide between personal ambition and service to others. Decide which number holds the key to your potential at this time, and work toward realizing that potential.

A QUICK GUIDE TO PERSONAL YEAR NUMBERS

1 *A time for new beginnings, personal and professional*

2 *Time to revise and strengthen what you have begun*

3 *A year for personal and professional development and achievement*

4 *Time for hard work, self-discipline, and application*

5 *A time of change*

6 *Learn from the past to plan for the future*

7 *A year for self-awareness and spiritual growth*

8 *Time to connect with your inner self and with others*

9 *Time to assess the past, and enjoy the fruits of your labors*

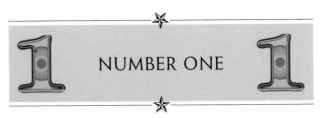

NUMBER ONE

Number one is associated with the Greek single-element monad, that means "divine spark," and represents the beginning of creation. Numerologists believe that in order to create the world, God invoked the power of the number one. Number one is also associated with materialism, the physical body, birth, and rebirth.

THE NUMBER ONE PERSON

⑥ *Qualities: Probably a pioneering extrovert who loves life. Number ones possess the qualities of leadership, creativity, courage, self-reliance, enterprise, energy, enthusiasm, generosity, diligence, and intuition. You take a single-minded approach* to setting and achieving goals. Number ones crave success, and the recognition and adulation that comes with it.

⑥ *Negative qualities: The downside of being a number one is that you can be dictatorial, resentful, aggressive, negative, dependent, and non-cooperative. You may also be fickle and selfish, boastful, and lazy.*

CAREER CHOICES

Number ones are leaders who have the ability to excel at anything that requires them to be courageous, bold, innovative, and creative. They make good inventors, producers, designers, directors, business entrepreneurs, and explorers.

CAMPAIGNER MARTIN LUTHER
KING HAD THE NUMBER ONE
ATTRIBUTE OF LEADERSHIP.

NUMBER ONE CONNECTIONS

Number one is linked to the color red. It is also linked to Monday, being the first day of the week. In astrology, it is associated with the Sun and Mars, and with the signs Taurus and Aries. In eastern energy medicine, it relates to the "chakras," or energy centers of the body. It has an affinity with the base chakra, the chakra of procreation, that is red, and the solar plexus or sun chakra, that is yellow.

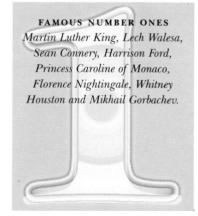

FAMOUS NUMBER ONES
Martin Luther King, Lech Walesa, Sean Connery, Harrison Ford, Princess Caroline of Monaco, Florence Nightingale, Whitney Houston and Mikhail Gorbachev.

NUMBER TWO

Number two is associated with the emotions. It is the number of unity, nurture, and sustenance. In the numerologist's view of creation, God divided the power and potential of the number one to create two, allowing creation to continue. It relates to opposition, but also to unity and complementary forces such as night and day, masculine and feminine. Number two is also linked to mental creativity.

THE NUMBER TWO PERSON

⊙ Qualities: Caring, communicative peacemakers. Gentle, diplomatic, receptive, wise, and tactful; number twos make very good listeners and mediators. You can be patient, cooperative, trustworthy, loyal, adaptable, sensitive, and cautious.

⊙ Negative qualities: You can be oversensitive and gullible, and may be vulnerable to shallow romantic attachments. You are often moody, melancholy, and unpredictable. You can be indecisive and muddled in your thinking. When not being cooperative you can be a troublemaker and you may even be overcautious to the point of being fearful.

CAREER CHOICES

Politician, lawyer, diplomat, social worker, counselor, healer, nurse, or any career where they mediate and act as a peace-maker. Their creative potential means that number two people make good writers, artists, dancers, and composers.

NUMBER TWO CONNECTIONS

Linked to the color orange, the color of propagation and divine love. Two relates to the navel chakra, the seat of the emotions and gut instincts, and to the heart chakra,

THE PRINCE OF WALES HAS THE ARTISTIC AND
DIPLOMATIC QUALITIES OF A NUMBER TWO.

the seat of sensitivity and under-standing. Astrologically, number two relates to the Earth and the idea of the Earth mother. It is also asso-ciated with the Moon, the mother of the world, and with the star sign of Cancer, the sign that governs the womb and fertility.

FAMOUS NUMBER TWOS
*Anne Brontë, Madonna,
Shirley Bassey, Mozart,
Prince Charles, Ronald Reagan,
Bill Clinton, and Diana Ross.*

3 NUMBER THREE 3

Three is the number of the mind. In ancient geometry it is linked to the triangle, the symbol of logic, intellect, and reason, and to the symbol of fire. In the numbered account of creation, God is believed to have called upon the power of three to give consciousness to his creations on Earth.

THE NUMBER THREE PERSON

☾ *Qualities: Number threes are pleasure-loving, enthusiastic, happy, generous, and full of life. You are creative, optimistic, and outgoing, you can be inspiring, communicative, caring, and adaptable.*

☾ *Negative qualities: A tendency to be a scatter-brained flirt. You can be superficial, extravagant, impractical, cynical, and a worrier. Your least attractive feature is a manipulative tendency, lack of focus, bad temper, and a tendency to cheat.*

CAREER CHOICES

This is the number of the self-expressing original thinker and creator. Threes make good writers, artists, comedians, and musicians. Any work that promotes or sells beauty and well-being, or uplifts people, such as the priesthood, dancing, and teaching, appeals to the number three person.

NUMBER THREE CONNECTIONS

Linked to the color yellow, the color of intellect, logic, and reason. The number three is connected to the solar plexus chakra which is the seat of the intellect and reason, and to the heart chakra, the seat of sensi-

PAINTING FULFILLS THE CREATIVE
NATURE OF A NUMBER THREE PERSON.

tivity and communication. The number three relates to Wednesday, as the third day of the week. The planets Mercury and Jupiter and the astrological sign of Virgo combine to make up number three's cosmic connections.

FAMOUS NUMBER THREES
Jane Austen, Salvador Dali, Indira Gandhi, Bill Cosby, Jayne Mansfield, F. Scott Fitzgerald, and Alfred Hitchcock.

NUMBER FOUR

Four is the number of will, determination, practicality, and the physical self. It is the tetrad symbolized by the square, that stands for equality and evenness, and the cross, a symbol of power and determination. Both are also strong earthing signs. According to numerological history, God called upon the number four for its power of will, needed to spur consciousness into action.

THE NUMBER FOUR PERSON

⊙ *Qualities: Fours are enduring, practical, motivated, responsible, reliable, and disciplined – you represent stability in life. You are neat, efficient, helpful, focused, and hard working. You have the ability to think logically and act with honesty, loyalty, and commitment.*

⊙ *Negative qualities: Greatest weakness is misguided will, that can make number fours impatient, careless, dominant, and violent. Your resistance to change can be marked negatively by intransigence, narrow-mindedness, and neurosis. With some fours "reliable" can mean dull, and motivation is inclined to give way to laziness.*

CAREER CHOICES

Physical and mental building work appeals to the constructive number four: farmer, miner, brick layer, craftsman, numerologist, astrologer, chemist, and financial advisor are careers that attract a number four person. Fours also veer toward campaigning and welfare work.

WOODWORKING IS LIKELY TO
SUIT PRACTICAL AND FOCUSED
NUMBER FOUR PEOPLE.

NUMBER FOUR CONNECTIONS

Linked to the color green and the planet Earth. Astrologically, attributed to the planets Mars and Saturn, and the sign of Virgo. It relates to Thursday, the fourth day, and its chakra is the red base chakra, the chakra of reproduction.

FAMOUS NUMBER FOURS
Dolly Parton, Sigmund Freud, Catherine Deneuve, Margaret Thatcher, Harold Wilson, John Major, Clint Eastwood, Arnold Schwarzenegger, and Demi Moore.

NUMBER FIVE

In many ancient cultures, the number five was revered as the number of vitality and life. It functions in a similar way to four, but on a collective, rather than an individual, basis. In the story of creation, God is said to have used the power of five to link the human with the collective will. Five is symbolized by the five-pointed star and the pentagon.

THE NUMBER FIVE PERSON

⑤ *Qualities: Fives are enthusiastic, clear thinkers. You are quick-witted, competitive, versatile, magnetic, friendly, passionate, sensitive, and popular. You adapt easily to change, and you will try anything new, often success-fully. Freedom-loving and adventurous, fives have a passion for travel.*

⑤ *Negative qualities: Have a tendency to be a Jack of all trades. Fives can be unfocused, indecisive, and restless, and can fear close attachment. Unhappy fives can be demanding, deceitful, hyperactive, and destructive ditherers. You can let your popu-larity lead you to fame and fortune rather than self-fulfillment.*

CAREER CHOICES

The communicator and collator of ideas, a five is best employed in adver-tising, as a lecturer, news-reader, writer, magazine editor, musician, investi-gator, or salesman. Fives also make good actors, interpreters, scientists, and researchers.

NUMBER FIVES LIKE TO TRAVEL
AFAR AND TO BRING IDEAS AND
INFORMATION TOGETHER.

NUMBER FIVE CONNECTIONS

Associated with the thymus area or spiritual heart, and with the fifth or throat chakra. Its color is sky blue, the color of communication. It relates to Friday, as the fifth day, and is associated with the planets Saturn and Mercury, and the sign of Libra.

FAMOUS NUMBER FIVES
Abraham Lincoln, Charlotte Brontë, Claudia Schiffer, Marlon Brando, Mick Jagger, Andre Agassi, Rudolf Nureyev, Adolf Hitler, and Vincent van Gogh.

NUMBER SIX

Six is the number of wisdom, knowledge, harmony, and loves beauty and color – hence the "flower-power" of the Sixties. It is symbolized by a six-pointed star made from two interlaced triangles. God is believed to have used the power of six to impart wisdom and create harmony throughout the universe.

THE NUMBER SIX PERSON

⑥ Qualities: Sixes can inspire wisdom and understanding. You can be benevolent, loving, creative, generous, and compassionate. Sixes seek harmony, and are patient, steady, and graceful and often principled, philosophical, and intuitive. You seek meaningful relationships, are family-oriented, and concerned about others.

⑥ Negative qualities: Number six has a tendency to be excessively idealistic, impractical, jealous, and argumentative. When not the wise counselor, six can be an interfering nag. With lofty ideals sixes often resent service, and are conceited, bigoted, and vengeful. Sixes may also veer toward martyrdom and low self-esteem.

CAREER CHOICES

Six is the wise carer. Sixes are drawn to careers in teaching, nursing, medicine, counseling, social work, child minding, or baby-sitting, gardening, and farming. A six is happy in any occupation that makes life or the environment more beautiful.

PUBLIC-SPIRITED YET PROUD? AMERICAN
PRESIDENT NIXON DISPLAYED GOOD AND
BAD NUMBER SIX TRAITS.

NUMBER SIX CONNECTIONS

Linked to planet Mercury, and to
the star signs Gemini, Sagittarius,
and Aquarius. Six is associated with
the solar plexus chakra, that is the
seat of the intellect and reason, and
with the color yellow/gold, that is
linked to wisdom.

FAMOUS NUMBER SIXES
*Richard Nixon, Stevie Wonder,
Steven Spielberg, Meryl Streep,
Vanessa Redgrave, and
Glenda Jackson.*

NUMBER SEVEN

Seven is the number of unconditional love, spirituality, and mysticism. It is symbolized by two seven-pointed stars, a triangle within a square, or a six-pointed star within a circle with a dot in the center. In the numerological account of creation, God is believed to have used the power of the seven's love to unite and preserve creation.

THE NUMBER SEVEN PERSON

⑥ *Qualities: Sevens can be contemplative, sensitive, perceptive, introspective, and with a strong tendency toward spirituality. Often you are modest, analytical, truthful, wise – and are good at giving advice. Sevens have a desire to serve. You also tend to be observant, keep confidences, and have a great love of nature.*

⑥ *Negative qualities: Being loners and introverts, sevens can be emotionally cold to others, unwilling to accept criticism, and may become social misfits. You can also be secretive, and modesty can give way either to an inferiority complex or to arrogance. In number sevens, failure to achieve spiritual enlightenment can lead to overindulgence in physical pleasures.*

CAREER CHOICES

The perfectionist – engineer, healer, lawyer, astrologer, artist, academic, and scientist. Sevens suit any occupation that requires research for details and ways to make things work. Jobs that encourage service usually appeal more than those that make money.

SENSITIVE, SPIRITUAL, AN
ARTISTE — MARILYN MONROE HAD
MANY NUMBER SEVEN ATTRIBUTES.

NUMBER SEVEN CONNECTIONS

Linked to the colors blue and pink, the colors of communication and unconditional love respectively. Seven relates to the throat chakra, and Sunday is seven's day. Seven is also linked to the planet Saturn.

FAMOUS NUMBER SEVENS
Winston Churchill, Marilyn Monroe, Princess Diana, Jean Shrimpton, John F. Kennedy, Nikita Krushchev, Václav Havel, and Elle Macpherson.

NUMBER EIGHT

Eight is the number of endeavor and of connections. The symbols of eight, the octagon and the eight-pointed star made from two squares, are both symbols of the self. The shape of the number eight suggests its purpose in creation as the circuit of energy, on which the spirit becomes physical, and the physical returns to the spiritual.

THE NUMBER EIGHT PERSON

Ⓖ *Qualities: Eights are realistic, ambitious, and energetic organizers. You have business flair, intelligence, and confidence, along with the determination, and leadership qualities necessary to build a successful career. Intuitive – even psychic – and analytical thinkers, eights are also honest, tending to be home-makers and providers.*

Ⓖ *Negative qualities: Eights can be proud, stubborn, unforgiving, and materialistic. You have a ruthless streak and can misuse power. You are also inclined to be impa-tient, weak-willed, snappy, and immoral. Eights also tend to worry and bicker, be lacking in spontaneity, and be intolerant of other people.*

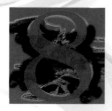

CAREER CHOICES

Eight is the organizer and analytical thinker. Careers in science, finance, building, supervising, manufac-turing, law, the army, and police all appeal. Eights are also drawn to clairvoyance, psychology, medicine, and healing.

EIGHT — PABLO PICASSO'S
NUMBER — IS CONNECTED TO THE
PLANETS ASSOCIATED WITH THE ARTS.

NUMBER EIGHT CONNECTIONS

The colors magenta and indigo are linked to eight, as are the navel chakra, and the brow chakra. Eights are linked to the "arty" planets of the Sun and Jupiter, and to the star signs Capricorn and Sagittarius.

FAMOUS NUMBER EIGHTS
Elizabeth Taylor, Oscar Wilde, Picasso, Joan Collins, Nancy Reagan, Barbra Streisand, Liza Minelli, Ginger Rogers, Saddam Hussein, and Neil Armstrong.

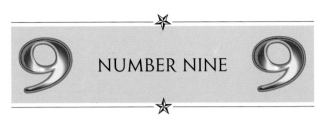

NUMBER NINE

Nine is the number of law, balance, and completion. It is symbolized by three interlaced triangles, which is the sign of perfection and completion. In the numerological account of creation, God used the power of the number nine to finish His work.

THE NUMBER NINE PERSON

◎ *Qualities: Nines are humanitarian, self-controlled, broad-minded leaders. You are creative and intuitive teachers. Nines love balance and harmony. You are caring, sharing, wise, spiritual, and happy-go-lucky, but with a sense of duty.*

◎ *Negative qualities: May be selfish, subservient, and a law unto yourself. Lack of balance can bring out aggressive, destructive, critical, and resentful traits.*

Nines can be vain, power-hungry, and praise-seeking gluttons.

CAREER CHOICES

The visionary. Teachers, preachers, scientists, artists, and surgeons, nines travel far and are drawn to any occupation that improves the world.

NUMBER NINE CONNECTIONS

Related to the color white and the black/white relationship. Nine is linked to the brow chakra, known as the third eye, and its color, indigo. Nine is associated with Mars and Neptune, the planets of curiosity and understanding, and star signs Sagittarius and Pisces.

FAMOUS NUMBER NINES
Orson Welles, Dustin Hoffman, Mahatma Gandhi, Brigitte Bardot, Shirley Maclaine, and General Franco.

THE NUMBER NINE RELATES TO PEOPLE WHO SEEK TO CHANGE THE WORLD, SUCH AS PRIESTS, DOCTORS, SCIENTISTS, AND ARTISTS.

MASTER NUMBERS

11 is the number of spiritual insight and revelation as well as intuition, symbolized by the 11-pointed star and associated with the planet Uranus. When the number 11 is too difficult to live up to, the digits can be added together and turned into a two.

THE 11 PERSON

⑥ *Qualities: Eleven is intuitive and idealistic. You can be patient, honest, capable, sensitive, and spiritual. Eleven loves the arts, has high expectations, and is humanitarian. This person is an inspirational teacher who nurtures and listens to others.*

⑥ *Negative qualities: Can be oversensitive, intransigent, and too choosy. May be impractical, temperamental, and impose too-high standards on others. Elevens can become unstable and dejected when their ideals are rejected. At worst you are lazy, socially inept, and have a tendency to project your own faults onto others.*

CAREER CHOICES

The inspirational writer, teacher, or religious leader. Elevens love the limelight, perhaps as an artist, actor, diplomat, politician, astronomer, New Age therapist, or astronaut.

SPACE WALKING MIGHT APPEAL TO
A NUMBER ELEVEN'S GRAND AMBITIONS
AND LOVE OF PUBLICITY.

The number 22 has no geometric symbol, but it has been linked to the planet Neptune. Twenty-twos have a desire to create a slightly better world than the one into which they were born. Twenty-twos can change their number to four if they find 22 is too difficult to bear.

THE 22 PERSON

© *Qualities: Imaginative, secretive, and perceptive, twenty-twos seek balance and harmony, and possess an inner strength. You are powerful, organized, insightful, and logical – hard-working builders who undertake large projects. Twenty-twos are loyal, optimistic, and can often be exceptionally generous benefactors.*

© *Negative qualities: Can be pessimistic and have an inferiority complex. When cynical and destructive, you only half-finish tasks. Sometimes you are selfish and manipulative. Unstable twenty-twos make cruel and fanatical tyrants.*

CAREER CHOICES

This is the number of master achievers. The organizer and public advisor, humanitarian, ambassador, and mediator between organizations and people would be ideal career choices. The facilitator who turns dreams into reality – engineer, architect, developer, or secretary.

TURNING A PLAN INTO A FINISHED BUILDING IS THE SORT OF JOB THAT IS IDEAL FOR A 22 PERSON.

NEPTUNE'S DESTRUCTIVE
EARTHQUAKES SYMBOLIZE THE
WORST OF A 22 CHARACTER.

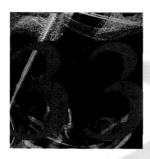

CAREER CHOICES

The 33 person is perfect for a job of service to the community of the world. Thirty-threes are attracted to roles in caretaking, childcare, wildlife, and ecology. They are often nurses, doctors, therapists, and counselors.

The most difficult number to bear, 33 is the number of unconditional love and martyrdom. Thirty-threes can choose, instead, to turn 33 into a six if they find the number too demanding.

THE 33 PERSON

☉ *Qualities: The 33 person is often a healer, a warm, caring nurturer, and a psychic. You can take on the worries of the world and fight for the underdog. Children are very much drawn to their love.*

☉ *Negative qualities: Thirty-threes can be negative, destructive, and afraid to heal themselves and others. You can also be interfering, and yet never have time when others need you. There is a tendency to wallow in your own misery and always to play the martyr. Thirty-threes can attract the weak-willed and those who take advantage.*

WITH HER MISSION TO HEAL AND WORK FOR THE POOR, MOTHER TERESA IS A TYPICAL 33 PERSON.

THE CARING 33 PERSON IS DRAWN TO
OCCUPATIONS INVOLVING ANIMALS AND ECOLOGY.

CONCLUSION

You should now have a sound under-standing of the power and potential inherent in numbers. They have more significance than simple religious interpretation, as was thought by scholars and clergymen such as St. Augustine. Giving us valuable insights into our personality, our strengths, and our weaknesses, numbers can offer guidance throughout our lives and help us attain greater success and fulfillment.

NUMBERS HAVE MORE THAN
JUST THE RELIGIOUS
MEANING ST. AUGUSTINE
BELIEVED THEM TO HOLD.

A SEVENTEENTH-CENTURY ARTIST SHOWS THE COSMOS'
MULTIPLICITIES, THAT NUMEROLOGY INTERPRETS.

FURTHER READING

BECK, Lilla, and HOLDEN, Robert,
What Number Are You? (Thorsons,
1991)

COOPER, D. Jason, *Understanding
Numerology* (Aquarian Press, 1996)

PRINGLE ADAMSON, Meg, *Know
Yourself Through Numerology*
(Headline, 1995)

USEFUL ADDRESSES

THE CONNAISSANCE
SCHOOL OF NUMEROLOGY,
Research House, PO Box 131,
Fraser Rd, Greenford, Middlesex,
England.
Tel: 0181 810 5644

*For details of the International
Association of Numerology, contact the
Connaissance School.*

INDEX

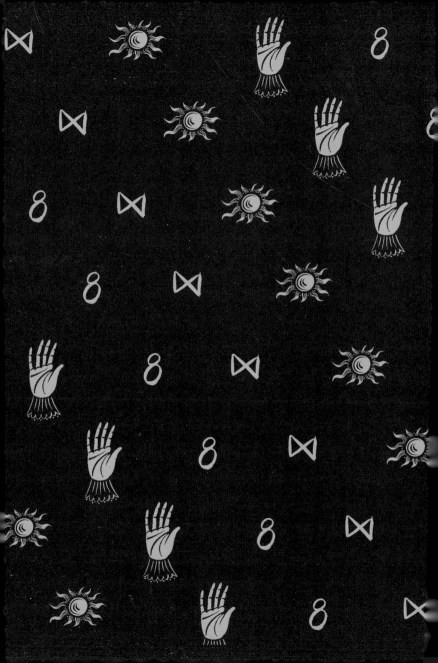